To Zander, Sarah, and Penelope

the contemporary
guesthouse

the contemporary guest

edizioni press

susanna sirefman

house
building in the garden

in town

in the countryside

at play

in private

By Invitation Only

The contemporary guesthouse is fundamentally a modern innovation. A building typology largely unknown before the last century, the guesthouse is today as much a symbol of luxury as it is an extension of hospitality. In the 21st century, domestic privacy is considered an intrinsic human right, essential to our personal well-being. Yet privacy is a cultural invention. Our collective (primarily Western) conception of privacy within our homes—in particular, the notion of individual sleeping quarters—has evolved considerably since the Dark Ages. In early Medieval European castles from the 1100s to 1200s, nobility would retire side by side with friends, family, and guests in the same cavernous Great Hall where they had just feasted. Everyone was together in this one great room, although rank and lineage determined where in the open-plan space each person slept. According to medieval historians Joseph and Frances Gies, visiting lords and ladies would bring their own curtained strip-leather and timber beds, wooden tubs (also housed and used in the Great Hall), and an average entourage of 24 valets and 30 horses.

In the 13th century, increasing affluence combined with a desire for nighttime seclusion led to the development of separate upstairs chambers for the resident lord and lady. These rooms were often fitted with peepholes hidden behind wall decorations, known as "squints," from which an attendant could monitor the activity below. Very grand or royal figures usually slept in separate bed-suites shared only with ladies-in-waiting or stewards, who, as the bodyguards of the Middle Ages, were also on the lookout for trouble.

Domestic solitude was not a top priority for city dwellers either. Family townhouses doubled as family workplaces. These residences featured living space that functioned by day as a place of commerce (a storefront, bakery, factory, or counting house), and by night as a lodge for a vast array of family, apprentices, laborers, servants, and visitors. It was not until the 17th century, in Europe and Colonial America, that the private dwelling, a building typology dedicated to purely domestic activities, took hold. This was a direct cultural result of the increasing separation of family and work. As the complexity of Western society grew, the differentiation and separation of space according to function became accordingly elaborate. In well-to-do family homes, certain rooms were reserved for important occasions while others were for everyday use. Social and cultural codes largely defined how an upper or even middle class home functioned. By the 18th century, the notion of individual sleeping arrangements had become well established, and children, servants, and guests all had their own defined zones. As a consequence of this segregation of space, special arrangements, both spatial and social, arose to accommodate visitors and guests. The protocol for such visitors and houseguests ultimately became quite intricate. Gender and class defined who could use what and when. For instance, in the mid 19th century, it was the custom that after dinner men only would retire to a smoking room for coffee, liqueur, and cigars, while the women would take demitasse in their own drawing room.

During the 19th century in much of upper class England, Europe, and the States, the family seat, usually a grand country home, became the center of the owner's social life. House parties became de rigeur among a certain crowd. As travel took a lot longer then, guests would usually stay for lengthy visits, sometimes for months at a time. In the United States visiting friends and relatives were housed in guest suites within the mansion. Occasionally a freestanding building would be built as part of a compound to accommodate overflow or antiquated notions of propriety. At the exquisite Hyde Park Vanderbilt estate (along the Hudson River), for example, a large Greek Revival pavilion (with two full-time employees) was built in 1895, designed by McKim, Mead &White to house only single male guests who attended the many winter weekend balls.

By the mid 20th century, the idea of a separate guesthouse on exclusive properties had become quite popular. Essentially cottages in the garden, these buildings were an ideal marriage between the garden folly and a functioning domicile. Numerous celebrated modern architects have used these little buildings as laboratories, places to try out new design and construction ideas. A few examples of these important early Modernist guesthouses follow.

The renowned architect Philip Johnson built his primary residence, the iconic Glass House, in 1949 on a spectacular (now) 40-acre estate in New Canaan, Connecticut. A steel and glass box, the design was greatly inspired by Mies van der Rohe (with whom Johnson studied at Harvard). The project is a quintessential International Style Pavilion-in-the-Park. A deceptively simple transparent house set at ground level, it celebrates the surrounding rocky hills and forest. Johnson's intention was to control nature with thick glass panels in the classical "machine in the garden" style, and to saturate the entire space with light and boundless views. Along a zigzag path several feet away sits a guesthouse also erected in 1949 (and remodeled in 1953). A brick rectangular volume, the guesthouse has only two small circular Brunelleschi-inspired windows. The polar opposite in aesthetic to the expansive, open Glass House, the Brick Guest House is opaque and claustrophobic, although quite private. Papered in pink Fortuny fabric, Johnson used this little house to test configurations of vaulted ceilings, an architectural obsession that has continued to appear in much of his larger later works.

The great American Modernist Paul Rudolph, best known for his institutional buildings like the Yale Art and Architecture Building, began his career in the 1940s by designing residences in Florida. These early explorations include several guesthouses for middle class clients that are marvelous experiments with new materials and post WWII naval technologies. One of the best examples of these Floridian guesthouses is the Healy Guest House, or Cocoon House, built in 1950 in Siesta Key. A simple, geometric volume raised above the ground and cantilevered out over the water, the project has a hanging roof designed to employ a flexible vinyl compound used by the U.S. military to insulate ships. The curved roof caps an interior ventilated by walls that are enormous louvers; each wall can be opened or shut, either letting in delicious cross breezes or enclosing the inhabitant in a warm, cozy cocoon. This small but rich project clearly influenced many of the architects in this book. In fact, the Compound on the Gulf of Mexico I (page 156), designed by Toshiko Mori Architect, is a guesthouse annexed to a 1957 Paul Rudolph house.

The negotiation of an eloquent dialogue between guesthouse and existing main house is a difficult architectural design challenge. If the existing house is an important architectural icon this mediation is all the more formidable. In 1987, Frank Gehry, (probably the world's most famous living architect—a household name after designing the Guggenheim Bilbao, completed in 1997) designed the Winton Guest House near Lake Minnetonka, an annex to a home designed by Philip Johnson in the mid 1950s. The playful, sculptural, almost child-like guest cottage serves as a provocative counterpoint to Johnson's cool, austere, rectilinear house. The guesthouse is composed of six separate geometric volumes, rectangular, square, trapezoid, wedge, and cone shapes, that are connected on the interior. No fenestration or doorway is visible from the original house—entry is only possible from the back of the pinwheel layout. This unusually molded building appears significantly smaller than the monolithic Johnson house because of its piecemeal, fragmented, individually clad volumes. Finnish plywood, sheet metal, stone, and brick (which echoes the Johnson house) sheath the various building blocks that make up the cottage. With hindsight, one can see that the project clearly foreshadows Gehry's sculptural and textural preoccupations. A historically dramatic conversation is taking place between these two very different houses on a typical lawn in suburban Minnesota.

The recent fashion of building guesthouses now means that such structures are frequently included in the original program of a modern country home. Rem Koolhaas (the other international architectural star) incorporated separate guest accommodations into his plan for Maison à Bordeaux, a concrete home built in France in 1998. The main house was designed for a wheelchair-bound client and his young family so the formal entryway is through a landscaped courtyard with a spiral ramp. Across this courtyard and opposite the three-story main house sit two separate single-story volumes, the caretaker's house and a guesthouse. Half above, half below the ground plane, the guesthouse has its own private front entrance off the roadway.

Lesser-known contemporary architects also covet guesthouse commissions. The small scale and limited program of the guesthouse offers a rich testing ground for the architect and client. The intimate nature of a guesthouse requires a true understanding of form, proportion, light, and materials. While the guest cottage has an inherently simple program and therefore a simpler structure than the main house, the new edifice must strike an appropriate aesthetic and experiential balance between building and nature. Whether set in Italy on a sprawling coastline retreat or stationed on a suburban Australian back lawn, the on-site positioning of these mini-houses is of vital importance. The new structure must forge a meaningful physical and metaphorical connection with the larger house, as well as relate to the surrounding landscape.

Brian MacKay-Lyons, an emerging architect in Nova Scotia, Canada, has recently designed several projects that include miniature versions of the main house as a guesthouse. His recent House #22 (completed in 1998), built along a dramatic coastline, follows a simple parti: two identical cubic buildings, one big (the main residence) and one little (the guesthouse) are connected along a north-south axis. Both glass, corrugated metal, and concrete block structures are clad in local hemlock siding, and, despite being very sophisticated buildings in a pared-down Modernist lexicon, they give the charming appearance from a distance of a Mommy and Baby building.

Today, the building of a guesthouse on a private estate offers the perfect solution to the perennial house-guest dilemma. After all, everyone enjoys entertaining visitors but sharing personal space with house-guests (for any length of time) can be rather trying. The erection of a new self-contained dwelling, designed just for company, accommodates everyone. For both homeowners and guests, such a solution provides proximity without the loss of privacy. Personal boundaries are much easier to establish and maintain when they are delineated physically.

This book features 33 carefully selected contemporary guesthouses from around the globe. It is not intended as a comprehensive survey of all recent guesthouses, but rather it showcases a cross-section of projects that possess a high degree of architectural merit. All built within the last half-decade, these sophisticated little buildings cover a dazzling variety of styles, budgets, settings, and sizes. The common ground among these diverse projects is the employment of clean, precise, and rational tenets of contemporary Modernism. From Maison du Divorce, the reinvented garden shed in Normandy, France, to the extravagant fairytale Playhouse in Greenwich, Connecticut, each and every one of these projects was designed by architects who ascribe to a minimal yet luxuriant aesthetic. And indeed, better than any hotel can do, all the projects included here provide the host with much desired privacy, and houseguests with a comfy home away from home.

In the Countryside

All of the guesthouses featured "In the Countryside" are situated on expansive, dramatic sites that vary greatly. These spectacular private estates range from the Gold Coast House, set in the rough and ready Australian outback, to Podere 43, built on the bucolic Tuscan coast. Yet despite this diversity of landscape, all the buildings have one thing in common: they are domestic designs that blur the boundary between inside and outside.

The notion of incorporating local nature into domestic architecture can be traced back to the work of America's great Modernists, architects such as Frank Lloyd Wright, Richard Neutra, and Rudolph M. Schindler. Best known for his residential work in California in the 1920s and '30s, R.M. Schindler once wrote about the future of the house: "The garden will become an integral part of the house. The distinction between the indoors and the out-of-doors will disappear."

Of course, the manner in which a building relates to its landscape is entirely dependent upon the kind of terrain surrounding it. Lake/Flato Architects, the designers of the Pine Ridge Residence in East Texas, have so embraced the magnificent, relentless verticality of the surrounding Piney Woods, that they designed visible structural supports for each of the project's four pavilions as enormous upright timbers. Deep in the foothills of the Appalachian Mountains, a mild (but wet) climate allowed Mack Scogin and Merrill Elam Architects to cleverly manipulate architectural devices: porches, decks, and courtyards to frame outdoor rooms throughout the Mountain Tree House estate. An elevated deck, a significant element in this guesthouse, celebrates the verticality of the surrounding woods with its own manmade forest of bamboo stalks. The deck and courtyards define space but do not contain space. This guesthouse provides not only shelter but also a chance to relax and play within the surrounding nature.

Taking their cue from the remarkable vast manmade agricultural grid overlaid on this portion of the Italian countryside, the firm Labics utilized the pervasive geometry of the surrounding ploughed fields to inform their design of the guesthouse at Podere 43. Topographical lines created by an early 20th century farming process have been drawn into the project's plan, defining visual and spatial parameters, such as hallways and walls.

The dramatic capture of spectacular views, further erasing the border between interior and exterior, is also a common technique used in these diverse projects. Much thought clearly went into the careful siting and orientation of each guesthouse to maximize these panoramas, be they ocean views, a lakefront, or a sea of wild grasses. Innovarchi framed wonderful sea views at the Gold Coast House, and demarcated the interior public and private zones on the exterior of the building through the use of contrasting materials. The lower level of these two double-story stacked pavilions is solid, cool masonry while the upper levels are transparent glass boxes. A large sunshade verandah on the upper level creates a marvelous outdoor/indoor space appropriate for the sub-tropical Queensland weather and the client's desire to live out-of-doors.

Lake/Flato Architects
Pine Ridge Residence
BRUSHY CREEK, TX

Each separate pavilion in this complex is surrounded by trees.

← Tree poles support each building, mimicking the forest's verticality.

← Large expanses of glass provide spectacular lake views.

The Contemporary Guesthouse

↑ **The main living pavilion sports a screened-in dining area.**

↑ **Site Plan**

This weekend home in Brushy Creek, East Texas, sits on a magnificent 670-acre private forest that is bordered by a 100-acre private lake. The house was split apart into four independent pavilions in order to achieve privacy for both owners and visitors. The architects strategically placed each structure on this densely wooded site so that all inhabitants would have maximum privacy, minimum noise, and a spectacular view of the lake. The quartet of buildings consists of a main living space, a guesthouse, a bunkhouse, and a master suite pavilion. The main edifice, or living structure, is the programmatic and physical center of the compound, containing only public spaces: living room, dining room, kitchen, library, and screened porch. The three remaining pavilions are designed as sleeping quarters. Treating the site as if it were a campground, the architects metaphorically envisioned each structure as a glorified tent and did their best to barely intrude upon the ecology of the forest. Narrow flagstone and gravel pathways, landscaped to appear as though they always existed, link all the pavilions. An elevated wooden bridge connects the guesthouse and the bunkhouse, which sports three sets of bunk-beds.

In keeping with their sense of "green" responsibility, the architects were inspired by a local vernacular form: the lake house on stilts. Each jazzed-up cabin is supported, or more accurately, hung from tree poles of indigenous lodge pine. Hovering above the dense beds of pine needles minimizes the architecture's environmental impact while visually echoing the surrounding forests' verticality.

Located along the northern edge of this vast site, each pavilion has a private view of the lake. All southern elevations have large expanses of glass windows, or sliding doors with panoramic views. The northern façade of each building is clad in cedar siding stained a rusty red to match the woods. Both the main house and the master bedroom feature large screened porches overlooking the lake.

← The communal kitchen.

↑ The common living room.

A custom-designed fireplace and double chimney form the central core of the house.

The cylindrical grain silo (to the right) has been transformed into a Turkish bath.

The original farmhouse

on this site was built in the late 1930s as part of an extensive governmental scheme to rehabilitate the shallow, malaria-stricken salt marshes along the southern Tuscan coast. Known as Podere 43, the house got its name from a Dutch reclamation process the Italians adopted. This technique involves creating a grid of orthogonal embankments that are then drained, leaving large, square parcels of usable farmland segregated by low, regular ridges. In the 1930s, the architect Marcello Piacenti, popular with the fascist regime, was commissioned to design a grand master plan for this site in lower Maremma. True to the political sentiments of his time, Piacenti envisioned an agricultural utopia: a vast settlement of identical, self-sufficient, sequentially numbered farm compounds. Each complex in this bucolic worker's paradise would be a model mini-farm with stables, pigeon coops, pigpens, a dovecote, a cheese-curing house, a grain silo, a toolshed, and a bread oven. Podere 43 was one of 55 farms that actually got built.

↓ Site Plan

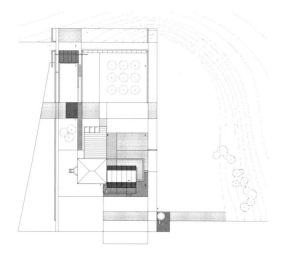

The architectural firm Labics converted the existing compound into an ultrachic weekend country home for a young couple with two children. The farmhouse, now the main house, was completely stripped down to bare limestone and then internally connected to what was once the barn. The resulting capacious central living core is focused around a state-of-the-art kitchen. The architects chose to demolish the majority of the surrounding outbuildings but converted the old pigsty cum outdoor meat curing shed into a luxurious guest apartment. Nearby, an old grain silo has been cleverly mutated into a Turkish bath.

The guest annex contains two bedrooms, a kitchenette, bath, and an entirely glazed sunroom. An existing platform roof and small porch that connected the pigpen and main house has been retained, preserving the original architect's intention: both spaces are separate and independent, yet part of the greater whole. In addition to Corten steel and a lot of glass (to make the most of the beatific pastoral views), local materials that weather well were used for the rebuilding: dry-laid stone from a nearby quarry for exterior walls, local sands as interior wall plaster, and floors that are either concrete or iroko hardwood.

A moat surrounds much of the house.→

← The architects used local stone from a nearby quarry.

← The living room hallway aligns with an original levee in the countryside.

↓ Section

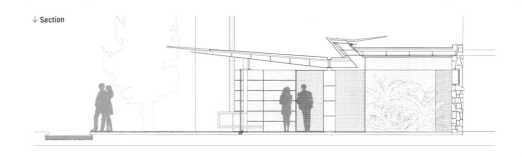

↓ The dining area and an
  interior courtyard
  between the main house
  and guesthouse.

The timber guesthouse is structurally supported by the stone garage.

← The guesthouse bedroom
opens directly to the
outdoors.

This guest cottage in Croton Reservoir, Upstate New York, was built about a year before the main house was erected, an unusual reversal from the more common practice of adding a guesthouse to an existing domestic property. The clients were eager to live on their site and it was quicker to build the more compact structure first. However, the architects, the Manhattan-based firm Archi-Tectonics, designed the two separate edifices, known together as the Gypsy Trail Residence, at the same time. The 1,500-square-foot guesthouse is intended to be the "alter-ego" of the 3,000-square-foot big house. It is similar in materials but is a smaller, simpler version of its more sophisticated "other."

Although set on a sprawling rural site, the interior of this cottage is an updated version of the suburban split-level house. A stone garage (composed of rocks found on site) supports the cantilevered wooden residence, which hovers marginally above the ground. One enters the elevated, slightly tilted structure through a set-back glass door that is protected by a fold of the building's wooden skin. A double-height living room leads to a slightly higher dining/kitchen area, which then leads onto a large, impromptu terrace on the garage roof. All public living zones are oriented toward the scenic lakefront, while the sleeping area has direct access to a private outdoor porch.

On the exterior, the building's striated wooden skin, has been cut at funky, unexpected angles creating an odd harmony with the surrounding craggy hillside. The stone base of the big house also supports a cantilevered wood, steel, and glass second floor. This volume has been slightly tweaked and twisted to procure a direct view of the lake and capture maximum sunlight.

← Sections

Particular attention was paid
to corner details.→

The subtly distorted geometry
of the north façade.→

Entryway to the main house.

↑ Common outdoor terrace.

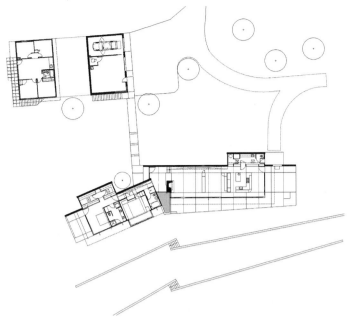

↑ Site Plan

The clients for this project, a semi-retired couple and recent empty-nesters, were intrigued by the privation of this six-acre site. Much of the land was scorched earth and the owners wanted to heal the landscape. Situated right along the banks of the Skagit River, their urban exodus was also driven by the desire to be as close to the river as possible. A dichotomous place, the site has two very distinct environments: the riverfront to the south and the wooded uplands to the north. A considerable amount of landscaping and planting was part of this project. The client's beloved rhododendrons were transplanted from their previous home in Seattle and a large pond was dug at the top of the property.

The design of both the main house and guesthouse grew organically out of these efforts to work the land. The architects, Weinstein AIU, designed a series of concrete walls that follow the contours of the land, and organize both the site and the built program. These vertical planes begin as low stone walls enclosing a series of terraced gardens, including an herb garden and a vegetable patch (the owners are marvelous cooks). The walls then serve as the spine and skylit gallery of the 2,600-square-foot main house. Providing a transitional element between the two natural precincts of the site, the walls ultimately disappear into the landscape at the guesthouse, enclosing the service space of the garage and shop, and providing a platform for the living/working space above. The 1,800-square-foot guesthouse is built into the hillside and faces the woods and manmade pond. The building is used as both a place for visitors to stay and the owners to work. This provides guests with privacy, and allows the owners to have physical distance from their home offices.

↓ Concrete walls serve as both edges and transitions.

↓ The garden is visible from this private entrance.

↓ The main house affords fantastic river views.

↑ Guests dine in the
main house.

All glazing is shaded
by retractable adjustable
aluminum louvers.

↑ The main cottage.

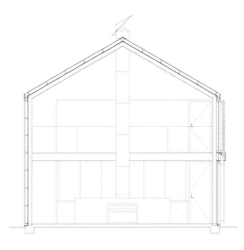

↑ **Section**

This guesthouse in the Southern Highlands

town of Mittagong, Australia (about one and a half hour's drive south of Sydney), gives new meaning to "living above the garage." The project is part of a small group of farm buildings including a main cottage and a converted cowshed that is now a potting shed. The guesthouse, a long low structure, occupies the site upon which the barn once stood and houses a capacious guest suite and home office, as well as machinery and tractor storage.

Set on the existing footprint of a demolished traditional barn, the completely new building replicates the height, roof pitch, and material of the original. This was not purely by choice but a requirement of the local Council. The big architectural difference between the old and the new barn is the contemporary steel structural system (rather than the original timber) that is visible both on the exterior and interior. The buildings' two-tone skin physically demarcates the barn's dual functions. The north and east walls of the barn, which house the domestic zone—a studio, living and dining area, bathroom, laundry, kitchen, library, and office space—are extensively glazed. The opaque, galvanized corrugated steel cladding on the western façade hides the work bays beneath. As the local climate can sometimes be quite harsh, all glazing is shaded by retractable adjustable aluminum louvers which when closed transform the shed into a totally sealed silver box.

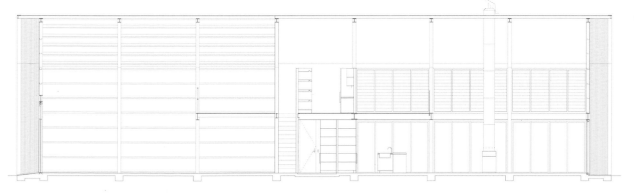

← **Cross Section**

Mack Scogin Merrill Elam Architects
Mountain Tree House
DILLARD, GA

A ramp provides access to
guest accommodations that
glow in the nighttime forest.

The Contemporary Guesthouse

← Bamboo sprouts
through the floor of
the outdoor deck.
↙ Deck handrails are
self-weathering Corten
steel and the floor is
black slate.
↑ The semi-enclosed
ramp leading to
the deck.
↓ The rear façade
of the ramp.

The Contemporary Guesthouse

"An inside-outside place," is how the designers, the husband and wife architectural team Mack Scogin and Merrill Elam, like to describe the Mountain Tree House. Blurring the boundaries between indoors and outdoors has been an obsession for them on this multi-phased project. Scogin and Elam were commissioned to design and build the main house five years before the 1,000-square-foot guesthouse and a 1,000-square-foot bamboo deck were finished. The original 4,100-square-foot Mountain House and a grand 900-square-foot porch sit long and low on this Appalachian foothill property in northeastern Georgia. The large main house seems even bigger as concrete walls cleave through the building, forming courtyards that define outdoor rooms, living spaces right smack in the forest.

The heavily wooded 24-acre site is a two-hour drive north of Atlanta and adjacent to a famous artists' colony. Bordered by a small stream, Barker's Creek, to the south (which supplies power for an old grist mill and water) and the North Carolina State Line to the north, the local terrain is a marvelous combination of mountains, hills, and fields. The architects spent a year merely surveying the property before siting the original house and orienting it toward the pasture. Probably the wettest place on the East Coast, the property has a unique microclimate. This required the main house and the guesthouse to be constructed on a raised concrete plinth. The Tree House is grounded by a concrete garage cum potting shed with a bedroom and playroom floating above amongst the vertical poplar trees. This transparent glass and steel structure then cantilevers out over a work-yard. The small adjacent steel-clad bathroom has doors that swing wide open for showers under the sun (or moon, perhaps). A long narrow deck set on thin steel columns juts out from the guesthouse, occupying space once intended to be a lap pool. Bamboo sprouting from planters on the ground shoots up through narrow slots in the black slate deck. Ideal for sitting, contemplating, reading, or engaging in water-play (as the client's grandbabies often do), the bamboo deck helps to blend the building into the surrounding forest. Although only 80 feet from the main house, the building orientation, elevated level, and the surrounding trees create the feeling of real privacy.

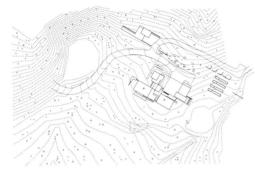

↑ Site Plan

← Detail of cantilevered guest bedroom.

← The guest bedroom interior looking toward the main house.

The guesthouse is nestled into an oak tree grove.

Sections → ↓

← The solid sandstone
 fireplace is the interior
 focal point.

← Echoing the main
 house, the guesthouse
 roof is copper.

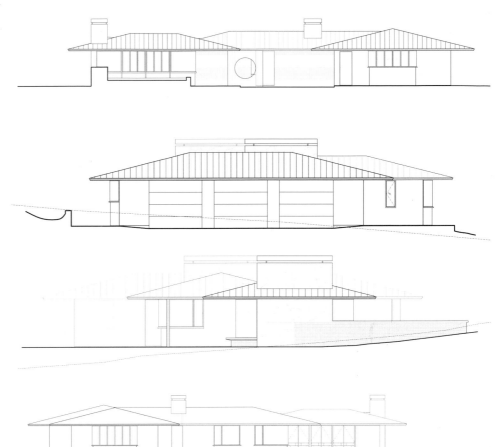

↑ Plan

The architects for this guesthouse, Shubin + Donaldson, took many of their design cues from the estate's existing mansion. The big house, dating back to the late 1930s, was designed by one of Frank Lloyd Wright's students at Taliesin West. The guesthouse, around 100 feet from the main house, is nestled among ancient, grand old oak trees. Shubin + Donaldson duplicated the horizontal form of the 4,000-square-foot original and topped their new glass pavilion with a matching copper roof. This allows the guesthouse to take full advantage of the five-acre property's gorgeous views of the Pacific Ocean to the south and the Santa Barbara Mountains to the north. In keeping with the tenets of the Prairie Style, the pavilion is anchored to the site by an enormous solid sandstone fireplace. This hearth wall extends beyond the borders of the house on either side.

← An abundance of
 glass melds the inside
 and outside.

← Plantings come right up to
 the edge of the house.

The upper floor deck is
an outdoor stage.

↓ The outdoor terrace is one long continuous plane.

Moveable floor-to-ceiling glass doors provide cross ventilation.→ ↘

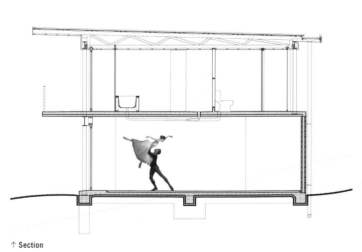

↑ Section

In the Countryside

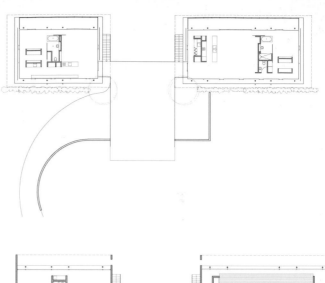

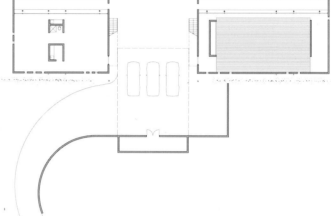

The client for this project, a world-renowned ballet teacher, had rather unusual requirements for her home: a state-of-the-art dance studio, an entertaining space, accommodations for her and her husband, a permanent self-contained apartment for her elderly mother, and a guesthouse for visiting ballet students and their parents. She also hoped to make the most of her elevated hinterland property and suggested the building be designed as, "a fishbowl with somewhere to get dressed." Capturing the 360-degree views of the high-grass, Queensland outback became of paramount importance to the architect's design of the house.

The building, on a sloping site facing the distant coastline, is divided into two double-story pavilions connected by a central entry platform. Living spaces for the client and her extended family are on the upper level, linked to the ground from behind and to all public spaces; an art gallery, art studio, guest suite, and ballet studio are located below. The upper floors, the project's private precincts, are essentially glass and steel boxes, in the tradition of Mies Van der Rohe's Farnsworth House. All services and enclosed rooms were placed away from the façade. Moveable floor-to-ceiling screens and walls offer temporary privacy when required. These large sliding panels and hinged walls modulate the use of the internal space to achieve the desired levels of separation between public, private, and intimate.

Full-height frameless laminated glazing was custom-engineered to maximize the sea view as well as to withstand tropical storms and cyclones. These glass façades are operable, sliding open to create wonderful north-south breezes. An expansive north-facing terrace runs the full length of both pavilions and is used for outdoor dance performances and cocktail parties. A large overhanging roof makes for a spectacular verandah, necessary in such a sub-tropical climate, known for temperatures well over 100 degrees Fahrenheit. Another integral part of the building's climate-sensitive design is the concrete lower level. The lower half of the building acts as a thermal mass, a cooling device for the upper floor in the summer and a warming device in the relatively mild winter. It is here, in the lower portion of the building, that students—who have traveled here from all over the globe to study ballet—live for weeks at a time, and dance on the sprung timber floor in the adjacent dance studio

↑ Even the house's bath-
rooms have a view of the
grassy outback.

In Town

The "In Town" guesthouse is an entirely different kind of enterprise than its countryside cousin. Space is at an enormous premium in the city. Even in the suburbs, extra turf is a rare and luxurious commodity. Therefore practicality takes precedence over frivolity, and functionality becomes a priority in urban guesthouse design. The majority of projects showcased in this chapter are multifunctional—they have been designed with added layers of program. Elliott + Associates Architects converted a 1920s vintage two-story servants quarters in Oklahoma City's Heritage Hills into a garage and guest suite. As the building is in a historic district, local zoning requirements allowed little manipulation of the exterior, so the completely gutted and redone interior became the main focus of the project. At 450 square feet, this petite guesthouse is a marvelously sensitive architectural exploration of light.

While urban zoning laws can often be restrictive, it was a zoning breach in Santa Monica, California, that was the catalyst for the design of the Guttentag Studio. Marmol Radziner and Associates were hired to bring the client's plot up to code—by building a two-car garage. The client's existing house, a 1945 prefab, was erected before a law was passed in the 1980s requiring on-site covered parking. The resulting, very modern garage and guesthouse/studio are now a local traffic stopper. In Chicago, Illinois, John Ronan Architect updated a turn-of-the-century carriage house by inserting a garage on the ground floor and designing a fluid space—a morphable living loft on the top floor. Layering of program and interior flexibility is critical to stretching space, getting the most out of every square inch. John Ronan pushes this notion, stating that "impermanence" was the inspiration behind the Perry Coach House. The guest apartment can be transformed at the whim of the user over the course of time: a day, a month, or a year. All program requirements have been cleverly camouflaged by streamlined millwork, allowing the open plan space to serve as a guesthouse, a playroom, a home office, or a small theater. Taking utilitarian innovation one step further, Daly Genik Architects designed a form-changing building at the Valley Center House in Southern California. Vertical and horizontal metal shutters placed strategically around the house enable the structure to expand and contract to accommodate a frequently fluctuating number of guests.

The need to negotiate a relationship within the fabric of the city is another complexity of city architecture. Gary Marinko Architects designed the Poll House in Perth, Australia, to turn its back on local clatter. The plan of the project is a series of separate color-coded volumes, including a guest suite, arranged around an interior courtyard. There are no windows on the side or street façades of this building—a clear indication that privacy is very important to the inhabitants of this house. Privacy was so important to the owners of the O'Neill Guesthouse in West Los Angeles, California, that Lubowicki•Lanier Architecture nearly buried the project at the bottom of their client's garden. Set on the lowest area of the site, at the bottom of a 26-foot slope, only the rooftops of the guesthouse are visible from the main house.

City or suburban dwellings tend to be primary residences, not vacation homes; therefore it is not a surprise that many of these guesthouses also include a home office. A home office outside the home is perhaps the ultimate luxury, the physical disconnection between the domestic world and the work world, affording a psychic serenity not possible when an office is next to the main bedroom. In Durban, South Africa, Elphick Proome Architects built an unusual guest pavilion with not one, but two dedicated office areas for the owners, a young couple. An egalitarian project, the steel-frame building has a reflexology studio for her and a study cum music room for him. The opposite (but related) urge, a desire to escape the office for a breath of fresh air, led Ross Anderson, founder of Anderson Architects, to erect a transparent tent on the rooftop above his workplace in Chelsea, Manhattan. An unusual hybrid of the guesthouse, this little tar beach campground (complete with an outdoor shower and communal firepit) is used for overnight stays, outdoor meetings, parties, and as an oasis above the city.

John Ronan Architect
Perry Coach House
CHICAGO, IL

Guesthouse exterior as seen from the garden.

The building's
original masonry shell
was retained.→

← A fold-out double bed is
hidden behind a panel.

← Here the millwork camou-
flages the kitchen.

The old juxtaposed against
the new.→

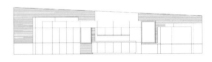

↑ **Floor Plan and
Corresponding Elevations**

In the posh Lincoln Park neighborhood, not far from the famous ballpark, Wrigley Field, finding a coach house behind a larger main house is quite common. More often than not these small buildings are used for storage space or maintained as garages. Architect John Ronan converted this century-old, two-story edifice into an elegant, self-sustaining guesthouse/work space for a young family. The carriage house is a 50-foot walk through the garden from the main 1890s graystone—the perfect urban setting for the client's visiting friends and in-laws.

The transformation began with the demolition of an attic hayloft and the removal of an old, broken-down Triumph TR6. The existing building had no weight-bearing walls on the interior—the entire structural load was carried on the exterior brick walls, creating a capacious loft-like space. Ronan was keen to retain the original brick and limestone shell, complete with picturesque wood joists and old fashioned square nails, for its historical resonance. The architect then handily exploited the existing open floor plan for maximum flexibility. An office, bathroom, and garage were inserted onto the first floor. The second floor was kept open-plan and transformed into a remarkably versatile living space underneath a new skylight. Hidden behind sleek, minimalist birch plywood panels are kitchen appliances, a Murphy bed, media electronics, and toy storage. Pulling up, folding down, opening, closing, or sliding shut various cabinetry around the perimeter of the room renders the space a conference room, playroom, hotel room, or kitchen.

Anderson Architects
Rooftop Night-Light
NEW YORK, NY

Against an ultra-urban back-drop, the translucent tent illuminates the city sky.

↓ The chimney of a wood-
  burning stove is visible
  penetrating the top of
  the tent.

The Contemporary Guesthouse

↑ Furry furnishings enhance
the tent's exotic ambiance.

If Clark Kent and Barbarella went camping together, their tent might look
something like this ultra-urban guesthouse. Perched atop the tar beach of an
industrial loft building in Chelsea, Manhattan, this project has a decidedly sur-
real undercurrent. The architect and owner, Ross Anderson, founder of Anderson
Architects, is a San Francisco native, and created this vamped-up Western-style
mini-campground as a decompression zone above his workplace. Accessed by
metal stairs through a hole cut in the ceiling of his office, the translucent tent, out-
fitted with a cowskin rug, fur bedspread, communal fire-pit, and outdoor shower,
are used by office staff, family, and visiting friends. Anderson occasionally sleeps
there, enjoying the "weird and odd cinematic experience." So far, though, none of
his clients have ventured an overnight stay.

Vertical strips of maple open onto the back of the property.

↑ The view from the main house down toward the stone patio and guesthouse rooftop.

The clients who commissioned this project requested that the architects design an unobtrusive guesthouse that was responsive to the landscape. The existing two-story house, an old Spanish-style bungalow several blocks north of Wilshire Boulevard, is on a deep, steep lot that, unusual for West Los Angeles, has a natural creek running through it. The architects placed the guesthouse on the lowest area of the site, 26 feet down, so that the stepped, terraced lot would cloak their intervention. Looking out from the main house only the guesthouse rooftop is visible.

Comprising the 800-square-foot guest apartment, a living room and bedroom stand as two separate architectural elements: a pair of cubes set deep within the garden. The two volumes, similar in size, scale, and proportion, are very different in materials and disposition. As though it were an army bunker, the stucco-clad bedroom is partly sunken underground. A slanted roof, planted with local reed grasses, gives the impression of the box slowly opening up.

Designed as an open structure in the garden, the exterior of the living room is a steel frame hung with horizontal copper panels, each separated by a two-inch strip of glass. These panels are mirrored with maple plywood panels on the interior, imitating the experience one might have inside an old upturned packing crate. The copper-clad roof is set at an angle, also slanted to let light in. A dining area, sheltered by the sloped ceiling plane, internally connects the two volumetric elements.

← Cross Section

↑ The stucco-finished guest bedroom.

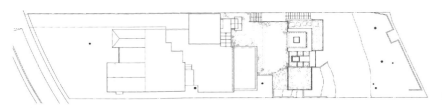

← Plan

The dining area. →

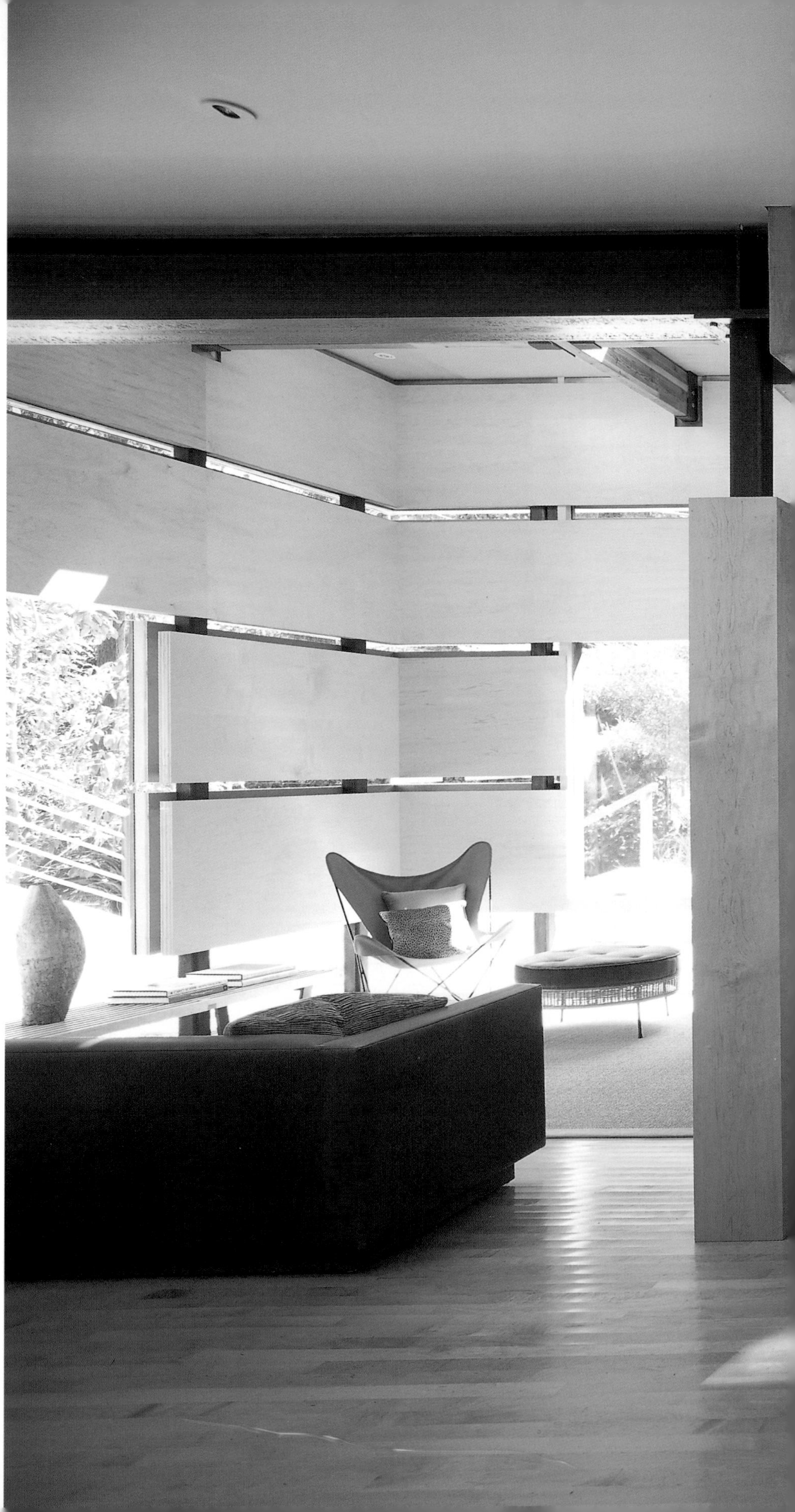

↑ The guesthouse roof
 is similar in shape to
 a bird wing.

↑ The guesthouse's indoor
living room transforms
into an outdoor deck and
dining area.

↑ Molding holes in the
concrete walls of the guesthouse have been retained to
provide cross-ventilation.

When viewed from behind, this studio/guesthouse in Durban, South

Africa, looks like an enormous, strange, and colorful bird resting on the back lawn.
It is the unusual form of the building—a floating metal (Zincalume) roof curved over
a steel framework that sits atop a series of interlocked brightly colored concrete
volumes—that creates this ornithological impression. The roof, morphologically
similar to a wing, curves gently upward, above the solid edifice below. The intersti-
tial space between roof and wall plane allows for a marvelous, light, and airy interior
with natural cross-ventilation, much appreciated in this hot, humid climate. Internal
glass louvers, high-level vents, and small, visible perforations (molding holes) in the
concrete walls allow the valley breezes to cool the building down. All these operable horizontal elements are sheltered by the broad overhanging roof, which, when
opened, transforms the entire pavilion into a lightweight verandah. The impression
of guesthouse as wildlife is enhanced by the building's thin connection to the
ground: the pavilion sits on a podium with attached hardwood-clad steel-framed
decking that seems to hover dreamily in the landscape.

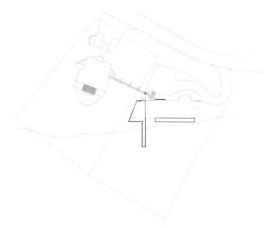

↑ Site Plan

The guesthouse was designed and built by George Elphick Architects 14 years
after designing and building the main house. Connected by a glassed walkway, the
new is designed to be "in dialogue" with the old. Individual his and her work studios
accommodate the architect owner and his reflexologist wife. The rest of the house's
program is entertainment-oriented: a guest suite and kitchenette, a music room, a
spacious indoor lounging area, and the outdoor deck, dining, and barbecue area.
African carvings and a large collection of South African oil paintings dot the custom-designed interior, which is richly appointed with indigenous woods such as
bubinga, balau, and African rosewood.

The eclectic landscaping strategy juxtaposes the natural bush forest with a typical suburban manicured lawn.

Entertainment zone. →

Outdoor dining area. →

Marmol Radziner and Associates
Guttentag Studio
SANTA MONICA, CA

The guesthouse is stacked at an unusual angle above the garage.

Exterior stairs lead to both the guesthouse and the main house.

The Contemporary Guesthouse

← The guesthouse opens onto
  a small garden.

↓ The deck has a terrific
  view of the Pacific.

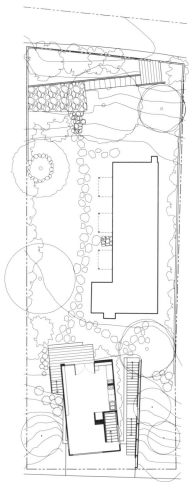

↑ Site Plan

Set on a steep and compact slope in Santa Monica Canyon, this charming little guesthouse is jam-packed with activity: a two-car garage, studio, guest room, entertainment space, and open rooftop terrace. The 2,000-square-foot project grew out of the owner's need to satisfy a local Los Angeles mandate requiring on-site covered parking for all such properties. The existing house, a 1945 prefab, was built long before this law was enacted in the 1980s. The owner, a young single man, saw this as an opportunity to expand his 1,000-square-foot house by building a domestic venue for visiting friends to hang out.

The new freestanding design is essentially two stacked rectangular volumes that have been embedded into the hillside. The two volumes have different orientations, creating a very avant-garde aesthetic. The concrete block, lower level car park is parallel to the street, while the contrasting redwood-clad upper volume is twisted to align with the existing garden. The twisted 36-foot-high (the maximum allowed) house and roof terrace maintain the client's uninterrupted view of the Pacific Ocean and prevent a view directly into the next door residence. A stone path leads nine and a half feet through a small garden from the old to the new.

The interior is simple
and flexible. →

In Town

View from under the covered
walkway. The main courtyard
is in the foreground and the
pool is to the left.

Living and dining room illuminated by kitchen walls.

↑ Bedroom courtyard looking
   toward the retreat.

↑ Dining area.

↑ East passage toward the bedroom courtyard.

↑ Entrance passages.

Skylit living room with
glowing light walls.

East passage with guest suite
in the foreground.

Street façade at night.→

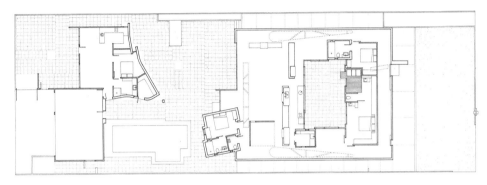

Plan →

On a typical suburban subdivision in Nedlands, Perth, sits a very atypical home. Poll House, a minimalist, concrete-paneled building, is a stark contrast to the surrounding overenthusiastic Italianate "McMansions." Sunken several grades lower than its next door neighbors, the understated house, rather subversively, has no fenestration on the side and street boundaries. A corrugated metal oversized hipped roof seems to be the only nod to the local architectural more: "size matters."

The house is effectively three residences: one house for the owner, guest accommodations, and a small granny flat. It was necessary to level the site to accommodate the client's wish that the house be fully wheelchair accessible. The resultant lowered ground plane meant that access to light through the walls on the east, west, and south elevations was severely limited. Gary Marinko Architects solved this problem by bringing light in through the roof and designing the project around a series of north-facing interior courtyards. Concrete retaining walls around the perimeter of the lot define the main internal circulation route that flows around various volumes within the house. These enclosed or semi-enclosed pods are color-coded: concrete for the two main bedrooms; blue-glazed brick for bathrooms, the guest suite, and the separate apartment; translucent fiberglass for the kitchen; and a segmented white cube for the study. The placement of these volumes is choreographed by the intensity of the sunlight that penetrates inside the space. The darkest rooms are the south-facing entry hall and bedrooms; the brightest are the public living spaces that are placed along the site's northern edge. To obtain maximum exposure to northern sunlight, the house needed to be as wide as the site would allow. Hence, the industrial materials palette—the most efficient and economical construction method for creating large open spaces—is that used in light industrial buildings: precast concrete and a steel roof system. On the interior the architects had some fun with traditional notions of artificial lighting as well. There are no light sources from the ceiling. Light is projected onto the concrete and glazed brick walls from hidden sources above cabinets, from fiber optics in the floor, and from within fiberglass walls.

← Entrance passage at night.

Original flue stack fitted with a slate panel for guests to write on.

Translucent partitions divide
the open plan guest loft.

Even the bedding is white.

← The guest apartment is
  located above the garage.

In the late 1880s the American government sponsored five Land Runs

in Native American territory, allowing white settlers to rush in and stake a claim to land. The well-known Territorial photographer North Losey was among these settlers and created a family homestead in what is known today as Oklahoma City's Heritage Hills. Losey's granddaughter, the owner of a 1920s Italianate mansion on this site, commissioned Elliott + Associates Architects to convert the adjacent freestanding servants' quarters to a garage and guesthouse.

Inspired by their client's famous ancestor, the architects set out to create a space that would be, in their own words, "what it is like if you are inside a view camera." As the building is landmarked (part of an historic district), the exterior was barely modified. New windows and garage doors were installed and the façades were reclad with gunnite. In keeping with their Modernist sensibilities, the architects replaced the exterior wooden stair with steel grates. But it is the interior of the tiny, 450-square-foot guest apartment that allowed Elliott + Associates Architects to experiment freely with light. The building was completely gutted. A garage was inserted on the ground floor and a one-room living space created on top. This open plan space is punctuated with a set of floor-to-ceiling glass-enclosed containers, called "vessels" by the architects. These four vessels, purposely placed in front of windows, define four distinct programmatic functions: entry, closet, bathroom, and bedroom. The sandblasted translucent glass of these dividers is a natural filter for daylight, allowing both time and climate to color the space accordingly. At night, halogen lamps cause the vessels to glow. An old stove flue grounds the center of the white open-plan room. A square white column with a small glass reveal at the base connects the two floors and allows a peek into the garage below.

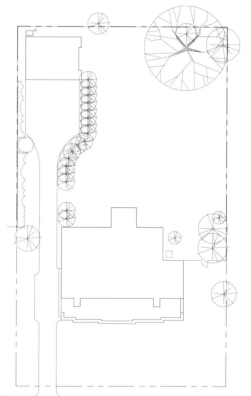

↑ Site Plan

→ Perspective View

114

Rock walkway and guesthouse.

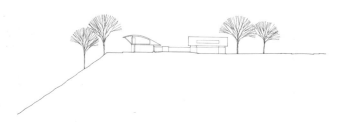

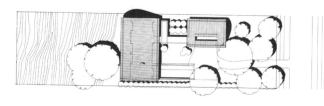

↑ **Site Section & Site Plan**

The architects for this project, Weinstein AIU, began work by razing the entire site. With the kind of detail that goes into planning major cities, a comprehensive master plan replete with even a laundry pavilion was drawn up for this "tabula rasa." A single-family residential compound, the layout is for a 4,500-square-foot main residence, 1,500-square-foot guesthouse, garage, laundry pavilion, and greenhouse. A driving force behind the design of the L-shaped complex was the client's wish to minimize the size of the buildings; they did not want the plush compound to look too ostentatious.

Buildings fill the edges of this plateau site—the one-bedroom main house is located at the top of the property (sitting atop a cliff) while the other facilities are built along the northern perimeter. An interior garden court is at the center of the compound. In an effort to reduce the sense of enclosure, the one-bedroom main residence is almost entirely transparent. Sweeping views through the double-height ground floor kitchen and dining area reveal the proximity of Puget Sound and the dramatic Olympic Mountains. One climbs a spiral staircase to reach the two-bedroom guesthouse. Both buildings are capped by elegant zinc-clad roofs, which resemble the wings of an airplane. A considerable 12-foot overhang provides year-round weather protection while defining the transitional exterior spaces.

The architects used local
materials.

→ The large wooden deck is an important outdoor element.

A platform bridge across the reflecting pool connects the deck to the landscape.→

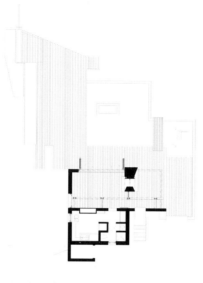

↑ **Floor Plan**
↑ **Site Plan**

This elegant pavilion

alongside a lush ravine in Toronto has a contradictory personality. It is designed to be used as either a secluded guesthouse or, at the opposite end of the spectrum, as the stage-set for elaborate parties. A sitting room with a sleeping area, kitchen (suitable for a couple of visitors or for catering large parties), and bathroom make up the interior. A sheltered outdoor dining area leading to a large wooden deck—inset with a reflecting pool that sports water lilies, bulrushes, and fish—extends the livable space of the project by half. Dotted around the deck are long concrete countertops that hide containers of firewood and are perfect for extensive entertaining. A wood-burning indoor/outdoor fireplace anchors the project, acting as both a visual and physical focal point. The rooftop of this project is quite unique. Shim-Sutcliffe Architects, well-known for their sleek use of new and local materials, devised a special system to incorporate structural glass channels into a steel frame that is hung from the roof by stainless steel cables. These glass channels create a continuous upper band of transparency, bringing light into the space and allowing the roof plane to float.

The guesthouse is
visually and physically
centered around an indoor/
outdoor fireplace. →

126

Daly Genik Architects
Valley Center House
VALLEY CENTER, CA

The site, in the foothills of Mt. Palomar, was selected for its western orientation and steep topography.

← Screens along each bedroom wing open to the landscape.

← These metal bifold screens completely seal the house when shut.

↑ Sliding walls and folding Murphy beds allow the number of bedrooms to vary.

↑ ↗ **Double-height dining area and kitchen.**

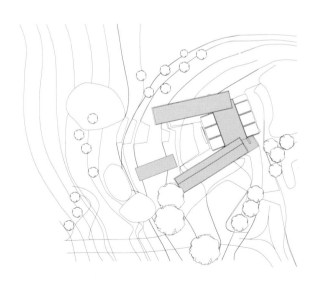

↑ Site Plan

This rugged, 2,800-square-foot residence in the foothills of Mt. Palomar is the primary home of a retired citrus rancher. The building is also programmed as a guesthouse for the frequent and lengthy visits of the rancher's three grown daughters and their families. Expandable and contractible, the one-story house can grow or shrink according to the needs of the inhabitants. The entire structure is covered with shutters, some that move vertically up and down and others that pivot horizontally back and forth. Forming a U shape in plan, two wings of sleeping quarters flank a large entirely glazed living/dining room. This enormous 20- by 32-foot central glass box is screened from the San Diego desert's excess sunlight by the electronically retractable perforated aluminum shades that roll up and down much like a garage door. The two almost identical bedroom wings are shuttered on the north and south façades with perforated aluminum bifold doors that can be opened or closed according to the current user's needs. Opaque screens slide back and forth in the interior modulating the number of bedrooms in use from four to seven. Sliding panels also allow the sleeping quarters to be open fully to the outdoor paved courtyard and rectangular swimming pool.

The metal shell of the building provides a degree of fire protection. This was a serious concern for the owner as the new house replaces a more traditional ranch house that was destroyed in a wildfire in 1996.

At Play

This chapter is devoted to the hybrid guesthouse: huts, cabins, cottages, and pavilions that are programmatically multi-layered or, conversely, pared down and stripped of almost all functionality. Built to celebrate downtime, these guesthouses are dedicated to either serving particular sports activities or to providing relaxation and retreat. Sometimes the house may be conducive to the pursuit of both. The holiday homes included here represent a diverse cross-section of recreational activities: skiing, hiking, biking, swimming, sunning, and relaxing. Two of the works featured, the Greenwich Playhouse and the Pavilion on Long Island, do not provide sleeping quarters. Strictly speaking these are not guesthouses. They have been included here as natural extensions of the guesthouse and as terrific examples of building within the garden. They share a common preoccupation with all the projects in this entire book—an obsession with the landscape.

Austin Patterson Disston Architects' marvelously baroque Playhouse in Greenwich, Connecticut, is a modern-day pleasure house. Although the aesthetic of this luxurious funhouse is contemporary modernism, the building's relationship to the surrounding landscaped lawn and garden was greatly influenced by Italian Renaissance villa traditions. The processional experience of walking from house to playhouse is central to the design, and a bridge, steps, ramps, and meandering pathways all allow several means of access. The Pavilion, designed by Thomas Phifer and Partners, is pure contemporary whimsy. A reinvention of the ornamental garden folly often found in Europe's 18th century picturesque garden estates, there is a delightful (and intended) element of discovery when approaching the playhouse. Set quite far from the main house across an expansive field, the steel and wood pavilion sits on a grass lawn sheltered within the lee of an old oak tree. Like a tree house, the upper stories can only be reached by ladder. To get to the Martin Boathouse & Bridge located on the shores of Lake Austin in Texas, Andersson•Wise Architects designed a 200-foot wood and steel cable suspension bridge that leads a half a mile away from the main house to a stone staircase that then descends 100 feet. Giving new meaning to "garden path," this half-mile hike through rugged rocky terrain is an important experiential element of the waterfront retreat.

Physical connection is just one of the many complexities that must be resolved when negotiating the relationship between an existing big house and a new guest cottage. Both the Compound on the Gulf of Mexico I in Casey Key, Florida, designed by Toshiko Mori Architect, and the Harris Pool House in Palm Springs, California, designed by Marmol Radziner and Associates, are adjacent to great architectural icons. The original celebrated houses were designed by the great modernists Paul Rudolph and Richard Neutra respectively. Great care and sensitivity was given to the new structures' historical context; appropriate siting, style, and even construction methods all help to establish a dialogue between the two buildings. The Harris Pool House was in fact built after the owners of the Neutra house had renovated it to its 1947 standards. Many of the modern recreational amenities they required were not appropriate to the old house and so they commissioned a haven for their contemporary conveniences such as an entertainment center, exercise room, and steam room.

Each and every one of the works in this chapter celebrates its unique location. Whether immaculately positioned on a manicured desert lawn in Palm Springs, California, or perched in the rugged wilderness of the Florida Keys or floating on the unforgiving waters of Lake Muskoka, Canada, each of these projects is in harmony with its place.

Andersson · Wise Architects
Martin Boathouse & Bridge
AUSTIN, TX

Large windows open fully to
allow diving into the lake.

View from hillside approach.

← Access is by a 200-foot-long cable bridge.

→ Screened open-air living room.

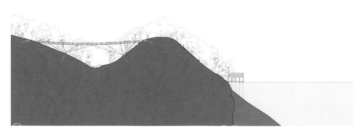
↑ Section

It is quite an adventure to traverse the extended pedestrian pathway leading from the main house to the boathouse on this residential estate in Texas. The half-mile connection includes a 200-foot cable-stay suspension bridge that crosses a deep ravine (reminiscent of a rope bridge in the jungle) to an opposite ridgeline that drops 100 feet via stone stairs to the boathouse on Lake Austin. The owners of the property commissioned Andersson•Wise Architects to design the new building and the means of access in such a way that they would have a "minimal impact on the landscape." The project succeeds in making a gentle, delicate mark on the rocky landscape and immerses the visitor in the vivid, verdant surroundings.

The two-story steel and wood boathouse shelters a covered boat slip, rowing scull, jetski slip, changing room, and an outdoor shower. The outdoor room on the second floor has convertible awning screens that open up overlooking the water. Two bays fully open to allow jumping or diving into the water. The vine growth on the farm-grown hardwood trellis covering the west and entry façades elegantly provides sunshade.

Cabin at twilight.

Mountains are visible
through the building.

An extra large
entryway accommodates
ski equipment.

Firewood stacked
against the building.

The guest suite is below the
guardrail.→

↑ **Galley kitchen.**

Eggleston Farkas Architects designed this vacation retreat for a couple and their grown children and grandkids who are frequent guests. In an attempt to maintain familial harmony during these holidays, the architects resurrected the once ubiquitous Edwardian house-planning convention of "upstairs, downstairs." At the beginning of the 20th century, in upper-class British homes, privacy and propriety (supposedly) were maintained through the vertical separation of staff and family: masters were housed upstairs while servants quarters were below. Here in this winter cabin, the owners have a large enclosed master bedroom underneath the peak of the sloped roof, while their guests have their own (rather nice) bunkhouse in the back of the house on the lowest level. Sunken four feet below grade to avoid the natural frostline. The capacious basement is filled with natural light. The galley kitchen, dining area, deck, and cozy living room are on the main level—considered communal space. The spare, efficient interior is perfect for reading, writing, and mapping out trails for the family's cross-country skiing and mountain biking jaunts. Windows frame various views of the valley: in the dining area a slot window reveals skiers passing by at eye level, the master bedroom has a wonderful expansive vista of mountains and trees, and through the glazed entryway one can see right to the other side of the building.

The wooden cabin is basically a sexy version of a local vernacular building type, the northwestern timber farm shed. Its sloped and slanted roof echoes the declivities of the surrounding terrain. In keeping with the entire project, the roof is both aesthetically pleasing and pragmatic: snow slides right off. The main entry stair, specially designed to accommodate skis and biking equipment, is artfully set below the roof and remains snow-free.

Entry to the guesthouse is via an exterior staircase.

Local hurricane code required the entire house be raised above flood levels.

↑ The exterior staircase
leads to an upper story
bedroom and rooftop
deck.

↑ **Living room.**

↑ **Floor-to-ceiling windows**
  and glass doors
  provide views and cross
  ventilation.

This romantic, remote estate, a 535-foot-wide sandbar south of Sarasota, is surrounded by water, dense vegetation, and extraordinary wildlife. To the west is the Gulf of Mexico, a protected sea turtle habitat, and to the east is Sarasota Bay, now a protected manatee habitat. The thickly planted site is exposed to dramatic climactic extremes: hurricanes, floods, downpours, and the blazing sun. But the estate's extraordinary natural context was not all the architect Toshiko Mori had to consider when designing the new structure, a guesthouse for the client's three grown children. The new building is an annex to a 1957 winter vacation home designed by the famous American Modernist architect Paul Rudolph. The existing postwar confection is a dynamic composition with cantilevered roofs and open-air living space. Close to a half century later, the 2,800-square-foot guesthouse, set on the footprint of a long-gone previous guesthouse, is a simpler, more contemporary, and more rigorous take on modernism.

Recent code required that the building be elevated above wave crest height, so the entire structure is on 17-foot-high pilotis. A full story above ground level, the guesthouse perches amongst the oak, palms, and mangroves which provide privacy and shade. T-shaped in plan, two separate and perpendicular pavilions house three bedrooms, three bathrooms, a living room, and kitchen. The smaller volume is two stories and features an open-air deck whose protective cantilevered roof plane mimics similar functional roof planes on the big house. An outdoor weatherproof stainless steel stair at the center of the plan connects and separates the activities within. The detached and suspended pavilions are faced with concrete block, fritted glass, and misty glass which is clear, opaque, or translucent as needed to protect from glare and heat gain. In homage to both the climate and to Rudolph's preoccupation with cross-ventilation, Mori has provided sliding glass windows and steel brise-soleil louvers that, when open, create effective cross breezes that help cool the building's one-room-deep interior.

Looking east toward the guesthouse and pool.

↑ The guesthouse has an independent driveway lined with cherry trees.

This seaside guesthouse in Long Island's tony Hamptons was designed by Hugh Hardy Associates in 1967. A miniature postmodern villa, the house was recently renovated and restored by its new owner. The main residence is a house designed by George Nelson on what was the adjacent lot. Stamberg Aferiat Architecture were called in after the guesthouse was essentially rebuilt to redesign the interiors. The owner requested they create a temporary home for his visitors that would, "Make me smile." The architects chose bold paint colors, classic modern furniture, joyous fabrics, and Pop Art of the same vintage as the summer house to create a bright and graphic interior.

↓ The hallway as seen from the dining area.

↑ The living room overlooks
an adjacent golf course
and pond.

↓ A David Hockney
painting hangs to the
right of a Stamberg
Aferiat–designed sofa.

The boathouse rests on the water supported by underwater piles.

View from Lake Muskoka.

The wooded pathway
to the boathouse.

To withstand local climate the building has a double-layered outer skin.

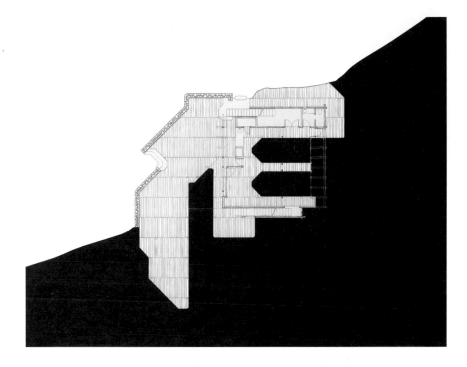

← Site Plan

The Muskoka boat

The Muskoka boat is a mahogany cruising boat indigenous to the Muskoka Lake Region, north of Toronto, Canada. Manufactured at Port Carling, the vintage 1930s design of these low and sleek polished wooden boats is particular to Lake Muskoka. This was the inspirational starting point for Shim-Sutcliffe Architects when designing a timber boathouse for an expansive waterfront estate. The new structure, which floats on the lake, provides two indoor 24-foot-long boat slips, an outdoor mooring, storage space for equipment, and a sleeping cabin above. The exterior of the building is constructed with stained heavy timbers: Douglas fir rescued from a demolished warehouse in Kitchener-Waterloo. As befitting a building set in such wilderness, the rooftop is part zinc and part moss garden.

The way in which the boathouse was erected on the lake also informed the design of this simple, elegant building. Local tradesmen fabricated the underwater infrastructure using traditional techniques appropriate for the rugged climate. A series of heavy timber cribs were made to form the building's foundations. This was done in the middle of winter when the lake was frozen; then, using chain saws to cut holes in the ice, the cribs—now filled with granite boulders that stabilize the structure—were sunk into the water. Once the winter was over and the ice melted, the house was built on top of these well-settled foundations. The timbers that surround the house are references to these foundations. This second structure within the heavy outer layer of the building is also evocative of a wooden boat. Stairs and the two outdoor porches have been inserted into these two layers of skin.

The interior has a nautical feel as well. The spectacular wooden ceiling is curved and much of the furniture and storage space is built in. The 650-foot bedroom has enormous windows and an elegant Japanese-style bathroom. Although simple, the boathouse is wonderfully luxurious. Every detail has been thoroughly designed, even reinvented. Almost all light fixtures and door handles were custom-designed and, to avoid stubbing toes on the dock, Shim-Sutcliffe designed a special boat cleat that could be installed flush with the dock.

← **The exterior docking area.**

The illuminated roof of the playhouse connects the party room with an outdoor terrace.

An elevated walkway connects playhouse and second floor of main house.→

On a sprawling estate in Greenwich Connecticut, 120 feet from an 11,000-square-foot International Style house, sits this extraordinary 2,793-square-foot playhouse. After completing renovations on the big house, Austin Patterson Disston Architects replaced an existing guesthouse on site with a multi-functional entertainment facility. Local zoning code required that the new structure follow the footprint of the demolished guesthouse. The clients, a couple and their four teenage children, requested two things: easy access to the new playhouse and that the materials used on the exterior echo the white stucco exterior of the Bauhaus-inspired main dwelling.

The freedom of the project brief and the rolling wooded hills, rocky outcroppings, orchards, and beautifully landscaped gardens on the property reminded the architects of 16th-century Italian villa architecture. Steeped in tradition dating back to Roman times, Italian Renaissance gardens frequently featured ornate pleasure houses that had no other practical purpose than to give pleasure. The fancy yet simple summer funhouses designed by the architect Vignola at Villa Lante and Villa Caprarola were of particular interest to the architects. These grand architectural precedents are both very much about the procession through the garden, movement from folly to folly. Therefore the experience of walking from the house to the playhouse became an important part of the Connecticut design. A 100-foot tubular steel elevated bridge connects the playhouse with the second floor of the main house; a stepped ramp and several meandering pathways provide ground level entry.

The asymmetric form of the giant, overhanging steel roof relates to the skewed axis of the original guesthouse footprint with the main house. The roof cantilevers over the playhouse's party room and a surrounding terrace. In addition to the party room, the playhouse has a media facility, an inglenook with a fireplace, an area for pool and ping-pong, a crafts room, a media workshop (the clients are computer buffs), and a tower with a lookout. The playhouse is literally not such a far cry from the Enlightenment Period—surely the owners must feel like royalty when viewing their domain from this lavish playhouse.

↑ Gameroom.

The Contemporary Guesthouse

↑ **Dining area.**

The pavilion is both sculpture and playhouse.

← A stainless steel
scrim serves as screen
and handrail.

Pavilion access is by
gangway ladder. →

Three hundred feet from a classic Long Island Sound clapboard house
sits this delightful folly. A cross between an art piece, a pavilion, and a playhouse,
this structure is often used for entertaining the owner's guests. Although this little
uncovered building is clearly not a full-fledged guesthouse, it serves as a well-
placed retreat for the owners, their two small children, family, and friends. It is the
perfect place to relax, serve drinks, and escape from the main house.

↓ Looking out from
the middle story toward
the woods.

The three-story transparent structure is nestled into a clearing beneath an old
oak tree, and affords spectacular views across the Great South Bay to Fire Island.
To reach the top level one must walk across a field and climb up the gangway ladder. The structure's mahogany frame is cross-braced by cables found in a local
boat-building shop, and functions as a counterbalance to the local wind condi-
tions. The two ends of the playhouse are solid wooden panels and help frame
the marvelous view. A diaphanous stainless steel scrim wraps around the second
story and creates the feel of a screened-in porch.

Salmela Architect
Emerson Sauna
DULUTH, MN

The triangular volume
houses the screened
cooling porch.

The forest surrounds the estate.

The building is a bold geometric composition.

Brick sauna chimney rises
from the sod roof.

The owners of this wooded lakeside property in northern Minnesota were keen to reinvent shared childhood memories of "Sauna Night." This was a Saturday evening tradition among local immigrant communities. Nostalgic for the weekly image of mellow chimney smoke rising from Scandinavian-American farmsteads across the countryside, they commissioned Salmela Architect to create a modern sauna on their estate.

The boldly geometric red brick structure (the building's strong form is evocative of the work of the late Italian architect Aldo Rossi) is located near the lake for quick dips between steamings. A very contemporary sauna, the interior of the building sports Philippe Starck fixtures, has in-floor heating for winter down time, and features a custom-designed sauna stove with glass doors that provide lighting for the steam room. A screened cooling porch acts as a private breezeway for cooling off "in the buff." Long wooden benches double up as places to cool off or as beds for overnight guests. The triangular cedar rooftop looks out onto the lake to the south and over the sauna's sod roof to the north. The sauna was tactically placed quite far from the large main house on site, in order to recreate the view of smoke rising from the chimney on "Sauna Nights."

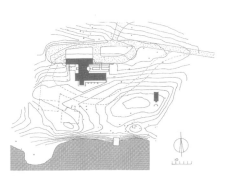

↑ **Site Plan**

Visual continuity between the old and the new was a priority for Marmol Radziner and Associates.

Looking back from the pool house toward the famous Kaufmann House.

Landscaping around the pool house celebrates the rocky local desert terrain.

The main house on this Palm Springs, California, site is a celebrated architectural icon. Designed in 1946 by the legendary architect Richard Neutra, the dwelling, known as the Kaufmann House (after the original owners), is a fine example of California Modernism. The image of this house is etched in America's collective consciousness because a dramatic photograph of it, taken in 1947 by the prominent architectural photographer Julius Shulman, became one of the most widely published images (first published in *Life* magazine) of this genre of architecture. The photo shows the house, pool, and mountains at twilight, and encapsulates America's post-war optimism.

Marmol Radziner and Associates spent four years, 1994 to 1998, meticulously restoring the Kaufmann House for its current owners, an architectural historian and a businessman, both of whom were passionate about the accuracy of the house and desert landscape restoration. During the process, both client and architects came to the conclusion that it was necessary to add a new building to the estate as a repository for the modern amenities the new owners desired. The new building houses a state-of-the-art audio-visual system, gym, steam room, small kitchen, and a flexible living space that is perfect for staging a large party.

Marmol Radziner were initially, "frightened to add a new structure near the Kaufmann House. We decided to create a framework to look back at the original house and to work with the attitudes Neutra established." In close proximity to the original structure (15 feet behind) and on an adjacent lot, the location of this new 1,200-square-foot structure was, in fact, informed by that famous Shulman photograph. The new building purposely frames the exact same twilight view through a large portal created by fully retracted sliding doors in the living room. Materials, construction techniques, and detailing all take their cue from the Kaufmann House, referring to the house without replicating it.

In Private

This chapter focuses on buildings that address varying cultural notions of privacy and proximity. Each project provides a unique, alternative (not always auxiliary) accommodation for both houseowner and houseguest.

The Residence for Art designed by Lake/Flato Architects in Dallas, Texas, is a new house on an old estate, adjacent to the original big house and a formerly converted carriage house. The ultimate guesthouse, this grand park pavilion was built by and for the most recent occupant of the big house. As though a permanent guest in her own home, the project allowed the owner an opportunity to build a house specific to her needs and vast modern art collection.

Maison du Divorce, in Normandy, France, is not only an avant-garde solution to hosting guests but offers a cheeky commentary on contemporary marriage. Designed with the assumption that "absence makes the heart grow fonder," this weekend home has a detachable, movable living/sleeping room for guests or disgruntled partners. Designed by two French architects, Fiona Meadows and Frédéric Nantois, this innovative house should make family get-togethers that much easier for all parties involved. The Bercy Residence in Austin, Texas, is not at all a guesthouse but a two-family residence. It has been included here because its layout—two separate, self-sufficient sleeping zones and a communal living quarters—resembles a guesthouse typology more than a two-family home.

In Japan, a combination of factors—city real estate is so dear, large properties are hard to come by, and cultural attitudes do not favor entertaining in one's urban home—mean that contemporary vacation homes are often built with the express purpose of hosting guests. Three projects in this section are all Japanese country homes, designed to provide for houseguests. It is remarkable how similar in aesthetic the Yomiuri Media Miyagi Guest House and the House on Mt. Fuji are. Respectively designed by Atelier Hitoshi Abe and Satoshi Okada Architects, both houses use flexible tatami rooms as sleeping quarters for their guests.

And finally there is the Picture Window House, a sublime piece of architecture designed by the celebrated architect Shigeru Ban. A full-time residence for a retired widower, the house is designed to accommodate his children who visit regularly. As with all projects in this book, the house and grounds are so beautiful, who wouldn't want to be a frequent guest?

The movable, plastic
walled living room.

The living room is
minimally furnished.→

The contained house
is ranch style. →

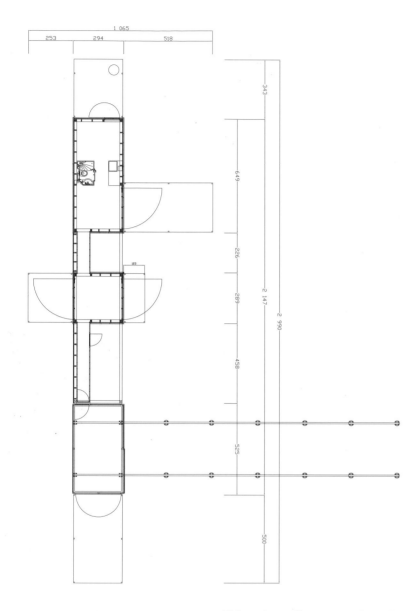

↑ **Plan**

This extraordinary country retreat built across two grassy trailer lots in Normandy, France, packs a double whammy in possibility. If the house's inhabitants require additional personal space from one another, the transparent living room can be disconnected from the ranch-style house and sent along a set of rails to rest 20 meters away. Mechanically operated by a low-tech crank and winch, the removable, double-height room travels along a pair of tracks to attach to an outdoor timber deck. Constructed of plastic, wood, and concrete, this modishly furnished weekend home looks like a playful reinvention of the garden shed. Not just an amusing and irreverent idea, the structural separation of one segment of the house actually creates a large outdoor room as well as an expanded sense of retreat, what the projects' architects, Fiona Meadows and Frédéric Nantois, call the "liberation of domestic enclosure." Put more simply, this project offers a getaway from a getaway!

Atelier Hitoshi Abe
Yomiuri Media Miyagi
Guest House
ZAO, MIYAGI, JAPAN

Interior of louvered porch.

Exterior of louvered porch.

↑ View of the dining/living
area and shoji screens on
upper level.

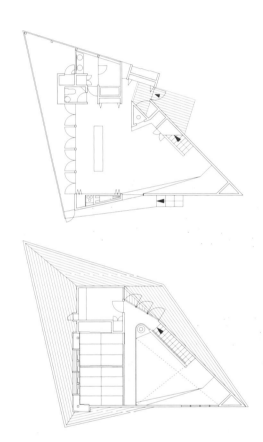

↑ **Plans**

Inspired by the way in which a kimono folds, drapes, and covers the human body, Hitoshi Abe, the architect of this quirky house, has created an architecture that folds over and around the landscape. An architectural transmutation of the hilly terrain, the building is folded, almost deformed, and, in some ways, becomes an extension of the forest. The louvered triangular porch is particularly successful as an ambiguous indoor/outdoor space.

Set on a spectacular site, the house is not far from an extinct volcano and adjacent to a national forest. An hour's drive outside of the city Sendai, the country house is used for both personal and corporate entertaining and education. The flexible interior can house just the owners and their visiting grandchildren, or be used as small conference center for parties of up to 30 people. The downstairs wide-open central living space can accommodate large groups, and two upstairs tatami rooms and a study can be quickly transformed into sleeping quarters for guests.

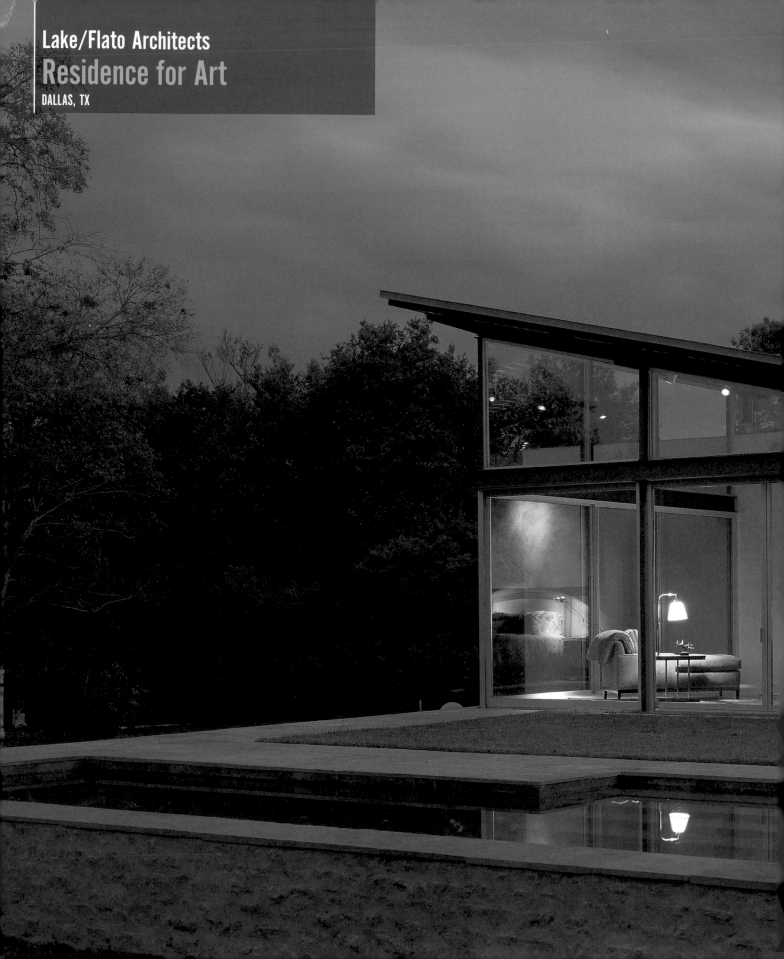

The butterfly roof rests on glass walls.

The sculpture garden
is visible from
the living room.→

↓ **Site Plan**

This remarkable house is adjacent to the owner's long-time residence—
an enormous 1930s mansion. The 6,500-square-foot lesser house (small only by
Texas standards) is truly a "pavilion in the park." Set catty-corner to the estate's
carriage house (which long ago was converted to an art gallery), the new house is
all about modern art. The owner had lived in the family's stately home for most of
her married life and as a widow since the 1960s. She was keen to have a house all
her own on the property. Located on four sloping acres, the residence houses a
master bedroom, living/dining area, kitchen, maids' quarters, and extensive gallery
space. The house is a T-shaped plan that incorporates a grand garden courtyard,
and, befitting the overall house theme, a perfect sculpture park.

The house is composed of two glass and steel volumes resting on a plinth that is
formed by two long masonry walls. Lake/Flato Architects describe these mortar and
limestone walls as the essence of the project. They are a contemporary interpretation of an indigenous building technique found frequently in Texas Hill Country.
The elegant stone walls define indoor and outdoor space, frame views, and control
natural light. Designed to be void of openings except at the top, they strategically
free up space for hanging art.

→ Gallery space.

↑ The dining area.

Depending on the light, the black-painted exterior blends into the site or stands out dramatically.

↓ A window at the end of the
hallway strategically
frames an outdoor view.

In Private

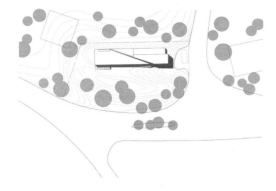

↑ **Site Plan**

The undulating black ground, black rocks, and black pebbles on

this site were formed by lava from Mount Fuji, a nearby active volcano. In response to this natural phenomenon, called "Fuji sand," Satoshi Okada Architects decided the exterior of this weekend villa 15,000 feet above sea level should be black. An enigmatic structure, the villa is a striking insertion in the dense 200-year-old forest, a national park. From some perspectives, the rectilinear house, clad in black-stained Japanese cedar, stands out dramatically against the green mossy lawn. From other angles, the dark building almost disappears into the lush magnolia, beech, and birch groves.

A country home near several celebrated golf courses, the house was built to lodge and entertain guests. The owners like to bring two or three families along with them when they come from Tokyo (about an hour's drive away) on weekends.

This 1,500-square-foot house is composed of two volumes, and it is unusual in that it is divided on the diagonal. One slice contains bedrooms, bathrooms and an eight-mat tatami room, while the other slice is programmed as living space with a large loft for parties, a dining area, and a kitchen.

→ Dining area.

This two-family home occupies a narrow downtown lot.

The house is constructed of an exposed modular steel frame infilled with prefab panels.

The house is constructed of an exposed modular steel frame infilled with prefab panels.

The Contemporary Guesthouse

← The roof deck has a
retractable canvas shade.

In Private

The Contemporary Guesthouse

← A water garden sits
between two separate
pavilions which
are connected by a
glass walkway.

↑ Bright blue acrylic panels
define the kitchen as a
separate volume within
the house.

Although designed as a two-family home, this unusual building in South Austin, Texas, programmatically resembles a main house with a separate guesthouse rather than two self-contained dwellings. Built for one of the projects' architects—a young single man—and his married brother and brother's family, the house provides just one shared kitchen, one living room, and one dining room.

The very modern house is on a narrow downtown lot, and takes the form of two steel-framed rectangular pavilions (at one- and two-stories-high) that are connected by a glass walkway. The larger family and communal living spaces occupy the slightly staggered lower level while the top layer is the architect's bedroom, a spare room, a bathroom and an outdoor roof deck. The two pavilions and the walkway are placed at the edges of the property allowing space for a stylish water garden set in between. This reflecting pool is the focal point of the house; all sides of the house open out onto it.

The architects for this project, Bercy Chen Studio, have a wonderful fresh approach to rather common materials. They have created voluptuous, evocative textures and surfaces throughout the house. For example, the service areas of the house—bathrooms, kitchen, utility room, storage room—are clad in sheets of boldly colored acrylic. Vivid bright blue walls and cabinets highlight the kitchen, and the upstairs hallway is a dramatic deep blood red. Several glass sliding doors allow entry into and egress from the house, but these are not ordinary glass doors. Huge by industry standards, these doors measure six by nine feet each. A spectacular trellis, made of a Brazilian hardwood, ipe, covers the front patio, serving as both a sunscreen and a beautiful architectural sculpture.

Shigeru Ban Architects
Picture Window House
IZU, SHIIZUOKA, JAPAN

The lower level has a clear span of 66 feet.

This extraordinary two-story house sits on top of a gentle hill look-
ing out over the Pacific Ocean. The site's rare, unobstructed panoramic view was
the driving force behind the design of the house. The project's architect, Shigeru
Ban, describes his initial reaction to the dramatic location: "The first time I set foot
on the site, my immediate response was to frame the wonderful view of the ocean
stretching horizontally. That is to say that the building itself should become a picture window. " And indeed this house is an enormous, inhabitable picture frame.

Two 66-foot-wide openings are book-ended by a double-height entrance with a
bathroom and a two-story pottery studio on the west and east respectively. These
volumes are the structural supports for the house which function (along with columns, beams, and diagonal braces on the upper story) like a bridge—allowing for
the enormous, wide open horizontal north-south span of the building. Living area,
dining area, and kitchen are on the ground floor where the floor surface melts into
an outdoor deck. This adjacent rail-less veranda, a modern interpretation of the
engawa, a common element in traditional Japanese architecture, further erases the
delightfully invisible boundary between outdoors and indoors in this dwelling. On
the ground floor, eight large (eight-foot-square) glass sliding doors provide shelter
(if needed) from the outdoors. A roof overhang provides shade on the deck while
the upper floor is shielded from excessive sunlight on the southern exposure by
exterior mounted aluminum Venetian blinds.

A full-time residence occupied by a retired widower, the (almost) 3,000-square-
foot home was designed to accommodate not only his needs, but the frequent visits
of his children. The upper level has four south-facing bedrooms (three of which are
for the owner's guests) and a long galley-like bathroom with five sinks, two toilets
and a bathtub. In a rather unusual layering of program, the hotel-proportioned lava-
tory functions as a hallway providing access to the bedrooms and a storage area.

↓ Indoor/outdoor living and
dining area.

↑ An upstairs bedroom.

↑ The second floor bathroom/
hallway.

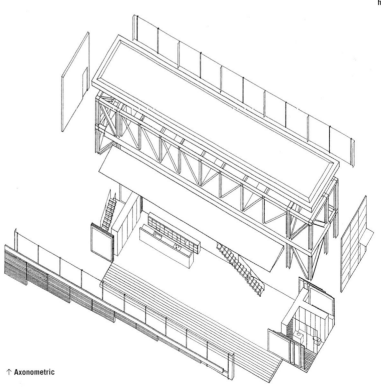

↑ Axonometric

Anderson Architects
Rooftop Night-Light
New York, New York
ARCHITECT: Ross Anderson, Anderson Architects, P.C.
CLIENT: Ross Anderson, Anderson Architects, P.C.
INTERIOR DESIGN: Ross Anderson, Anderson Architects, P.C.
LANDSCAPE ARCHITECT: Ross Anderson, Anderson Architects, P.C.
DECK CONTRACTOR: Site Management
TENT MANUFACTURER: Dave Ellis Canvas Products
PHOTOGRAPHER: Anderson Architects, P.C.; Pure+Applied

Andersson•Wise Architects
Martin Boathouse & Bridge
Austin, Texas
ARCHITECT: Andersson•Wise Architects
CLIENT: Tom & Mary Martin
INTERIOR DESIGN: Holden & Dupuy
STRUCTURAL ENGINEER:
Architectural Engineers Collaborative
CONTRACTOR: Four Corners Construction
PHOTOGRAPHERS: © Paul Bardagjy;
Andersson•Wise Architects

archi media – Fiona meadows + Frédéric Nantois
Maison du Divorce
La Chapelle sur Dun, France
ARCHITECT:
archi media – Fiona meadows + Frédéric Nantois
CLIENT: Mr. and Mrs. M.
INTERIOR DESIGN: archi media
LANDSCAPE ARCHITECT: archi media
CONTRACTOR: Mr. Villard
PHOTOGRAPHER: archi media

Archi-Tectonics
Gypsy Trail Guest House
Upstate New York
ARCHITECT: Archi-Tectonics, NY
CLIENT: Michael Spain
INTERIOR DESIGN: Archi-Tectonics, NY
LANDSCAPE ARCHITECT: Susan Lowry
STRUCTURAL ENGINEER:
Buro Happold Consulting Engineers
SURVEYOR: Bob Baxter
CONTRACTOR: Lydia Wusatowska of C&I construction
PHOTOGRAPHER: Winka Dubbeldam, Archi-Tectonics

Atelier Hitoshi Abe
Yomiuri Media Miyagi Guest House
Zao, Miyagi, Japan
ARCHITECT: Atelier Hitoshi Abe
CLIENT: Withheld at owner's request
STRUCTURAL ENGINEER: TIS partners
ELECTRICAL ENGINEER: Sogo Consultants
HYDRAULICS ENGINEER: Sogo Consultants
CONTRACTOR: Sugawara Construction
PHOTOGRAPHER: © Shunichi Atsumi

Austin Patterson Disston Architects
Greenwich Playhouse
Greenwich, Connecticut
ARCHITECT & INTERIOR DESIGN: David E. Austin, AIA,
Austin Patterson Disston Architects
CLIENT: Withheld at owner's request
INTERIOR DECORATOR: Gavin Johnston-Stewart
LANDSCAPE ARCHITECT: Wesley Stout Associates
STRUCTURAL ENGINEER: Edward Stanley Engineers
ELECTRICAL ENGINEER:
Nicoll Krepak Consulting Engineers
CONTRACTOR: Artisans, Inc.
PHOTOGRAPHER: Durston Saylor (interiors);
© David Sundberg/ESTO (exteriors)

Bercy Chen Studio
Bercy Residence
Austin, Texas
ARCHITECT: Bercy Chen Studio, LLP
CLIENT: Yannick & Thomas Bercy
INTERIOR DESIGN: Bercy Chen Studio, LLP
LANDSCAPE ARCHITECT: Bercy Chen Studio, LLP
STRUCTURAL ENGINEER: Structures by Jerry Garcia
SURVEYOR: Robert Barcomb
CONTRACTOR: Bercy Chen Studio, LLP
PHOTOGRAPHER: © Mike Osborne

Daly Genik Architects
Valley Center House
Valley Center, California
ARCHITECT: Daly Genik Architects
CLIENT: Withheld at owner's request
LANDSCAPE ARCHITECT: Daly Genik Architects
STRUCTURAL ENGINEER: Armando Paez
CONTRACTOR: Robert Lackey Construction
PHOTOGRAPHER: Undine Pröhl

Eggleston Farkas Architects
Methow Cabin
Winthrop, Washington
ARCHITECT: Eggleston Farkas Architects
CLIENT: Withheld at owner's request
STRUCTURAL ENGINEER: Jay Taylor
CONTRACTOR: Hall Construction
PHOTOGRAPHER: Jim Van Gundy

Elliott + Associates Architects
North Guest Apartment
Oklahoma City, Oklahoma
ARCHITECT: Elliott + Associates Architects:
Rand Elliott, FAIA + Michael Hoffner, AIA
CLIENT: Withheld at owner's request
INTERIOR DESIGN: Elliott + Associates Architects
STRUCTURAL ENGINEER: Lingo Construction Services
ELECTRICAL ENGINEER: Lingo Construction Services
CONTRACTOR: Lingo Construction Services
PHOTOGRAPHER: Robert Shimer, Hedrich Blessing

Elphick Proome Architects
Elphick Studio
Durban, South Africa
ARCHITECT: Elphick Proome Architects
CLIENT: George Elphick
INTERIOR DESIGN: George Elphick
LANDSCAPE ARCHITECT: Sibon Landscapes
STRUCTURAL ENGINEER: Martin and Associates
CONTRACTOR: A.P.M. Construction
PHOTOGRAPHER: Sally Chance and Craig Hudson

Engelen Moore
Hay Barn
Mittagong, New South Wales, Australia
ARCHITECT: Engelen Moore
CLIENT: Trish and Ian Hay
INTERIOR DESIGN: Engelen Moore
LANDSCAPE ARCHITECT: Nicholas Bray
STRUCTURAL ENGINEER: Peter Chan + Partners
CONTRACTOR: Eastwick Country Homes
PHOTOGRAPHER: Ross Honeysett

Gary Marinko Architects
Poll House
Perth, Western Australia, Australia
ARCHITECT: Gary Marinko Architects and the
University of Western Australia
CLIENT: Margot and Jaap Poll
STRUCTURAL ENGINEER: Bruechle Gilchrist & Evans Pty Ltd
ELECTRICAL ENGINEER: ETC Australia Pty Ltd
HYDRAULICS ENGINEER: Carrington Associates
QUANTITY SURVEYOR: Wilde and Woollard
CONTRACTOR: Cooper & Oxley Pty Ltd
PHOTOGRAPHER: Photographer John Gollings;
Jacqueline Stevenson;

Innovarchi
Gold Coast House
Bonogin, Queensland, Australia
ARCHITECT: Innovarchi
PROJECT TEAM: Stephanie Smith, Ken McBryde,
Ben Duckworth, Jad Silvester, Guilietta Biraghi, Torben Kjaer
CLIENT: Prudence Brown-Lennon and Richard Lennon
INTERIOR DESIGN: Innovarchi
STRUCTURAL ENGINEER: Rod Bligh, Bligh Tanner
GLAZING CONSULTANT: John Perry, Hyder Consulting
BUILDER: Rick Hering
GLAZING CONTRACTOR: Lidco
PHOTOGRAPHER: © Jon Linkins; Stephen Oxenbury

John Ronan Architect
Perry Coach House
Chicago, Illinois
ARCHITECT: John Ronan Architect
CLIENT: Withheld at owner's request
INTERIOR DESIGN: John Ronan Architect
CONTRACTOR: Eiesland Builders
PHOTOGRAPHER: Nathan Kirkman

Labics
Podere 43
Albinia, Grosseto, Italy
ARCHITECT: Labics
CLIENT: Withheld at owner's request
INTERIOR DESIGN: Labics
LANDSCAPE ARCHITECT: Olivia Collobiano
STRUCTURAL ENGINEER: Camillo Sommese, Studio 3S
ELECTRICAL ENGINEER:
Riccardo Fibbi, Carolina de Camillis
HYDRAULICS ENGINEER: Riccardo Fibbi
SURVEYOR: Gabriele Micozzi Ferri
CONTRACTOR: Indar SRL
PHOTOGRAPHER: Luigi Filetici

Lake/Flato Architects
Pine Ridge Residence
Brushy Creek, Texas
ARCHITECT: Lake/Flato Architects, Inc.
CLIENT: Withheld at owner's request
LANDSCAPE ARCHITECT: Rosa Finsley,
Kings Creek Landscaping
STRUCTURAL ENGINEER: Charles Lundy
CONTRACTOR: Don Romer, Rafter R Construction
PHOTOGRAPHER: Paul Hester

Lake/Flato Architects
Residence For Art
Dallas, Texas
ARCHITECT: Lake/Flato Architects, Inc.
CLIENT: Withheld at owner's request
INTERIOR DESIGN: Emily Summers Design AISD
LANDSCAPE ARCHITECT: Warren Johnson Landscape
STRUCTURAL ENGINEER: Goodson Engineering
ELECTRICAL ENGINEER: Basharkhah Engineering
SURVEYOR: PBS & J
CONTRACTOR: Tommy Ford Construction
PHOTOGRAPHER: Paul Hester

Lubowicki · Lanier Architecture
O'Neill Guesthouse
West Los Angeles, California
ARCHITECT: Lubowicki · Lanier Architecture
CLIENT: Donna O'Neill
INTERIOR DESIGN: Kay Kollar
LANDSCAPE ARCHITECT: Barry Campion
STRUCTURAL ENGINEER:
Parker/Resnick Structural Engineers
MECHANICAL ENGINEER: William Comeau
SURVEYOR: M & M & Co.
CONTRACTOR: Alexander Construction
PHOTOGRAPHER: Erich Ansel Koyama

Mack Scogin Merrill Elam Architects
Mountain Tree House
Dillard, Georgia
ARCHITECT: Mack Scogin Merrill Elam Architects
CLIENT: Withheld at owner's request
LANDSCAPE ARCHITECT: Marchant Martin
STRUCTURAL ENGINEER: Palmer Engineering
PHOTOGRAPHER: Timothy Hursley

Marmol Radziner and Associates
Guttentag Studio
Santa Monica, California
ARCHITECT: Marmol Radziner and Associates
CLIENT: Michael Guttentag
INTERIOR DESIGN: Marmol Radziner and Associates
LANDSCAPE ARCHITECT: Marmol Radziner and Associates
CONTRACTOR: Marmol Radziner and Associates
PHOTOGRAPHER: © Benny Chan/Fotoworks

Marmol Radziner and Associates
Harris Pool House
Palm Springs, California
ARCHITECT: Marmol Radziner and Associates
CLIENT: Brent and Beth Harris
INTERIOR DESIGN: Marmol Radziner and Associates
LANDSCAPE ARCHITECT (SITE INTERIOR):
Marmol Radziner and Associates
LANDSCAPE ARCHITECT (SITE PERIMETER):
Eric Lamers and William Kopelk
CONTRACTOR: Marmol Radziner and Associates
PHOTOGRAPHER: © David Glomb

Salmela Architect
Emerson Sauna
Duluth, Minnesota
ARCHITECT: Salmela Architect
CLIENT: Peter & Cynthia Emerson
INTERIOR DESIGN: Salmela Architect
LANDSCAPE ARCHITECT: Coen + Partners
STRUCTURAL ENGINEER:
Carroll Franck & Associates
CONTRACTOR: Rod & Sons Carpentry
PHOTOGRAPHER: Peter Bastianelli Kerze

Satoshi Okada Architects
House on Mt. Fuji
Yamanashi Prefecture, Japan
ARCHITECT: Satoshi Okada,
Satoshi Okada Architects
CLIENT: Sei Torii + Shunsuke Tomiyama
INTERIOR DESIGN: Satoshi Okada
LANDSCAPE ARCHITECT: Satoshi Okada
STRUCTURAL ENGINEER: Kenta Masaki
CONTRACTOR: Ide Construction Company
PHOTOGRAPHER: Hiroyuki Hirai

Shigeru Ban Architects
Picture Window House
Izu, Shizuoka, Japan
ARCHITECT: Shigeru Ban Architects
PROJECT TEAM: Shigeru Ban,
Nobutaka Hiraga, Jun Yashiki
CLIENT: Withheld at owner's request
INTERIOR DESIGN: Shigeru Ban Architects
LANDSCAPE ARCHITECT: Shigeru Ban Architects
STRUCTURAL ENGINEER: Hoshino Architect & Engineer
CONTRACTOR: Daido Kogyo
PHOTOGRAPHER: Hiroyuki Hirai

Shim-Sutcliffe Architects
Muskoka Boathouse
Point William, Ontario, Canada
ARCHITECT: Shim-Sutcliffe Architects Inc.:
Brigitte Shim & Howard Sutcliffe (principals),
Andrew Chatham, John O Connor (assistants)
CLIENT: Withheld at owner's request
STRUCTURAL ENGINEER: Atkins + Van Groll Engineering
MECHANICAL ENGINEER: Toews Systems Design
CONTRACTOR: Judges Contracting, Gravenhurst, Ontario
MILLWORK: Radiant City Millwork, Toronto -
Steve Bugler (principal)
CUSTOM FABRICATION: Takashi Sakamoto
CONSULTANTS: List Planning (planning)
PHOTOGRAPHERS:
Ed Burtynsky; James Dow; Howard Sutcliffe

Shim-Sutcliffe Architects
Ravine Guesthouse and Reflecting Pool
Toronto, Ontario, Canada
ARCHITECT: Shim-Sutcliffe Architects Inc.:
Brigitte Shim & Howard Sutcliffe (principals),
Min Wang, Mark Graham (assistants)
CLIENT: Withheld at owner's request
STRUCTURAL ENGINEER: Dave Bowick,
Blackwell Engineering
CONTRACTOR: Tony Azzevedo
PHOTOGRAPHER: James Dow

Shubin + Donaldson Architects
Carpinteria Guest House
Carpinteria, California
ARCHITECT: Shubin + Donaldson Architects
CLIENT: Withheld at owner's request
CONTRACTOR: Vision Builders
PHOTOGRAPHER: © Ciro Coelho/CiroCoelho.com

Stamberg Aferiat Architecture
Ranieri Guesthouse
Eastern Long Island, New York
CLIENT: Salvatore Ranieri
INTERIOR DESIGN: Stamberg Aferiat Architecture
(Paul Aferiat + Peter Stamberg)
ARCHITECT: Hugh Hardy and Associates
RENOVATION DESIGNER: Tiziana Hardy
LANDSCAPE DESIGN: Tiziana Hardy with Thomas Muse
CONTRACTOR: John Caramagna Builder Inc.
PHOTOGRAPHER: © Paul Warchol

Thomas Phifer and Partners
Long Island Playhouse
Long Island, New York
ARCHITECT: Thomas Phifer and Partners
PHOTOGRAPHER: Chris Callis; Steve Freihon

Toshiko Mori Architect
Compound on the Gulf of Mexico I
Casey Key, Florida
ARCHITECT: Toshiko Mori Architect
CLIENT: Betsy and Edward Cohen
INTERIOR DESIGN: Toshiko Mori Architect
LANDSCAPE ARCHITECT: Quennell Rothschild
STRUCTURAL ENGINEER: Stirling & Wilbur
CONTRACTOR: Michael K. Walker and Associates
PHOTOGRAPHER: © Paul Warchol

Weinstein AIU
River Residence
Skagit County, Washington
ARCHITECT: Weinstein AIU Architects + Urban Designers
(formerly Weinstein Copeland Architects)
CLIENT: Withheld at owner's request
INTERIOR DESIGN: Studio Frazar, Lisa Frazar
STRUCTURAL ENGINEER:
Magnusson Klemencic Associates, Jay Taylor
HYDRAULICS ENGINEER: Ecotope
SURVEYOR: Bowers West Land
CONTRACTOR: Nelson Lumber Construction
PHOTOGRAPHER: Lara Swimmer Photography

Weinstein AIU
Solbeck Residence
Seattle, Washington
ARCHITECT: Weinstein AIU Architects + Urban Designers
(formerly Weinstein Copeland Architects)
CLIENT: Withheld at owner's request
INTERIOR DESIGN: Weinstein Copeland Architects
LANDSCAPE ARCHITECT: Maggie Payne with the owners
STRUCTURAL ENGINEER: Ratti Swenson Perbix Clark
CONTRACTOR: Tom Paulson Construction
PHOTOGRAPHER: Michael Shopenn Photography

Acknowledgements:
Thank you to Anthony Iannacci and his staff at Edizioni
Press for inviting me to write a book on a topic of
my choice. It was great fun uncovering such a diverse
collection of global guesthouse projects. I am grateful
to all the architects included in the book, who were
so generous with their time and materials. I am truly
appreciative of their forward-looking clients without
whom these projects would not have existed.

A special thanks to the many photographers who
allowed us to publish their spectacular images
and finally, thanks to graphic designers Paul Carlos
and Urshula Barbour of Pure+Applied for their
elegant and imaginative book design.

First published in the
United States of America by
Edizioni Press, Inc.
469 West 21st Street
New York, New York 10011
www.edizionipress.com

ISBN: 1-931536-34-1

Library of Congress Catalogue Card Number: 2004115254

Printed in China

Design:
Pure+Applied
Editor:
Sarah Palmer

Cover:
Harris Pool House,
Marmol Radziner and Associates
Cover photograph:
© David Glomb

Back cover:
Compound on the Gulf of Mexico I,
Toshiko Mori Architect
Back cover photograph:
© Paul Warchol

Endpapers:
Emerson Sauna,
Salmela Architect
Endpaper photographs:
Peter Bastianelli Kerze

DATE D